How to Improve Your Memory

How to Improve Your Memory

Photographic Memory Secrets!

"Discover How You Can Unlock Your Mind's Amazing Natural Ability To Achieve A Photographic Memory - 100% Guaranteed...!"

Gain ACCESS To The Same Covert Methods That The Smart And Successful Have Been Using For Years...

DOWNLOAD NOW

How To...
MANIFEST A MIRACLE
Manifesting Reality Isn't Hard Work After All.
Discover My 100% Guaranteed Step-By-Step "Magic"
Formula To Manifest More Money, Love & Good
Health Than You Ever Dreamed Possible!
GARY EVANS
How To...
MANIFEST A MIRACLE
TRUE SECRETS OF THE MANIFESTATION PROCESS AND HOW YOU CAN PUT IT TO WORK FOR YOU
DOWNLOAD NOW
How To...
MANIFEST A MIRACLE

How to Improve Your Memory

Contents

Mental Exercises To Stimulate Memory Function

When you feel as though your memory is beginning to slip, there are certain exercises that you can use to stimulate your brain and get your memory back in gear.

One of the simplest methods is to read. Reading requires a good deal of concentration. Concentration is essential to memory function. By taking a few minutes out of each day to read you are stimulating your memory in a very positive way.

It doesn't need to be a book that you read. If news interests you than reading the newspaper during your coffee break is a perfect solution. This way you'll also remember the news stories that your colleagues or spouse might bring up and you'll feel confident having read the headline and accompanying story and then committing it to memory.

If news doesn't grab your attention, perhaps sports is more interesting to you. Imagine reading the scores of the games the night before and then being able to recite each one from memory. This not only feeds your sports craving it also stimulates your memory in a way that is really appealing to you.

Another fun way to get reading into your memory exercise plan is to read to your children. Children love this because it entertains them as well as allows them a few special moments with their parents. An added bonus is that while you are reading to them, it is also stimulating their memory. The words and the images in the book are something they enjoy and so naturally they want to commit it to memory. It becomes a wonderful association of learning and connecting with you.

Reading is a great exercise for the memory and when you read something that engages you it is almost effortless. While you are boosting your memory you are also boosting your knowledge database.

Boost Your Memory By Playing Bridge

Things have changed so much in our world that a simple game of cards is becoming a thing of the past. With the introduction of hand-held video games and computer software, picking up a deck of cards and sitting a table is quickly becoming a lost art.

Playing cards is a fun and easy way to socialize. It also can be competitive and it has another benefit that one might not notice at first glance. Playing cards are a wonderful way to exercise your mind and to boost your memory.

There are so many card games that are fun and easy. A few examples are:

- Poker
- Rummy
- Go Fish
- Bridge
- Hearts

Each is a bit different and many involve using your memory to get ahead in the game. Some games involve watching the cards closely and recognizing which cards have already been dealt and played. With a strong memory to work with you can almost guarantee that you'll have an advantage over the players whose memory isn't at the same top notch level that yours is. This can translate into a more challenging and rewarding game.

If you find yourself with a deck of cards and no opponents, a game of solitaire can offer the same memory boosting advantages as a rousing game of poker. Many games of solitaire involve close concentration and using your memory. Practice is said to make perfect and with solitaire that's very true. By developing concentration and memory skills you can beat the cards more than they beat you.

If you feel your memory slipping, picking up a deck of cards and dealing them out can help shift that memory back to where it needs to be. It's also a great way to strength concentration skills.

Learn A New Language And Boost Your Memory

When we are young most of us learn one language that we use for the remainder of our lives. Normally as we enter middle and high school we are required to take on another language. For many children they can pick up the basics of the new language fairly easily.

One of the fundamentals steps in learning a new language is committing the basic words to memory. Most of us know how to say hello and goodbye in French and perhaps even in Spanish. It's not because we learned how to read those words, but instead we heard them and committed them to memory. Remembering them when the time is appropriate we are able to draw them up from memory and pronounce them effortlessly.

Using this same technique to learn more words is not only a good way to further your vocabulary in that particular language but also to exercise your memory. This can be done at any age and the benefits to memory are just as important regardless of how old you are.

When you are in school, you take a class to learn a new language. In some cases this involves the use of diagrams and textbooks. You memorize the phonetic sounds and learn how to articulate the words properly. If you are older and looking to learn a new language you can do the same, attend a class or you can purchase a set of tapes that you listen to and mimic.

In the latter case, memory plays a significant role in learning the language because you are required to memorize the words and then recite them. While you learn each new word you are also committing it to memory. It's simply a great way to not only learn something new and interesting but it gives you a chance to boost your memory as well.

Music Can Boost Your Memory

Hasn't almost everyone at some point longed to be in a rock band? Or wished they were on the radio singing a country song while they strummed a guitar? Playing the trumpet or pounding out a beat on the drums. Having the ability to play a musical instrument whether it's the guitar, the drums or the piano is a great talent and beyond that a wonderful way to work on developing a strong memory.

One of the first steps to playing almost any musical instrument is to learn how to read music. For many people this seems like a daunting task. However it really just involves some basic understanding and the ability to commit that information to memory. Being able to read music is often equated to being able to ride a bicycle. Once you have the tools required to do it, you will always have the ability to do it. For reading music one of those tools is memory.

Once you grasp the notes you will then recall them from memory while you are learning to play a certain type of instrument. Many people once learning the basic notes can hear a song on the radio and play it without the written music in front of them. They are simply recalling the sequence of notes that has been embedded in their memory and using that to sound it out until it seems perfect.

The same principle lies behind our ability to sing along to a song we hear on the radio. Both the melody and the lyrics are within our memory and we call that up without thinking as we sing. Each time we do that we are exercising our brains and boosting our memories. This not only helps in the musical department but in other areas of our lives as well.

Cooking As A Cure To Memory Loss

Forgetting small things is common for most of us. Little things slip our minds and we become frustrated with our forgetfulness in the moment and then often even that feeling slips away.

There are certain techniques that we can use to give our memories a boost. Shifting them back to a place where they were sharp and alert.

A fun way to do this is to cook. Of course certain foods aid in helping with boosting the remembering power of your mind, but the act of cooking itself can be a great way to exercise your memory.

For many people cooking involves reading a recipe, gathering the ingredients and following the directions. That's a wonderful way of making certain that what you cook will be edible. It is however a great way to jog your memory back to a place it was years earlier.

The first time you cook a new dish, have the recipe book open. Follow the steps carefully, concentrating on each ingredient, the measurement of it and the directions for completing the dish. If it's a hit, then it's on to part B of the cooking to cure memory loss plan. The next time you whip up that dish for your family, keep the recipe book close but don't open it initially. Instead, gather the ingredients, and then check the book. If you've got them all, you've scored a point. The next part is easier, that's assembling them. Actions are an important part of boosting one's memory and since you can picture what you did last time, the steps should come to you easily. If you do get stuck, open the book and find the next step. Doing these steps several times on different days will help implant the recipe into your mind. Soon you'll be able to call that meal up from your memory with no effort at all.

Improving Memory Using Memory Exercises

For students preparing for different testes and examinations, struggling hard, would always need assistance with tricks to make their preparations and studies easier. Several students of different ages take advantage of knowing memory exercises. Teachers often make it a point to help students by telling them about various memory exercises they themselves implement since they began teaching.

Apparently, every person should use whatever appeals them the most. Methods working for one may not essentially work for the other. This could be demonstrated by a simple act of showing a child to tie up his laces. The child's concentration may go askew and end up in frustration when a new method of learning is suggested. Probably, one parent shows one way and at times grandparents disagree on best methods.

Distinctive methods

Young children with disabilities in learning need to know constructive methods to improve memory and have it tailored to one's own distinct capability. A struggling mind may need to associate few things with similar colors everyday for remembering. There would be shapes that helping them not to forget or even fragrances and odors. Children with bit of impairment might learn associating through scent or touches. For an instance grandparents may have selective perfumes or colognes worn daily.

Maintain consistency

Quite many times teachers have varied methods of teaching when compared to that of parents. When kids ask parents for assistance in their homework, arguments might develop as the parents' way to achieve a result would vary from the methods teachers use. If the child is taught to be silent and not to argue, by the parent, it could result in inefficient marks on whatever is turned in. Hence one should maintain the cooperation and consistency in a parent-teacher relationship.

Healing music

Have you tried making a silly and funny song about people who have offended you? This of course is a great exercise to your memory, though labeled as mean. Music is a great assisting substance essentially when it comes to teaching young kids about memory improving. This however must be reduced using is a disparaging manner. Many a time, comedians joke with impolite songs resulting in audience remembering the specific comedian just because the song acted as a substance to fortify the person into one's memory. You may not even recall the wordings, but just the tune as the results are all the same.

Games which rhyme are helpful tools for your memory. Millions of people have been brought up learning to enjoy antics the characters in stories of Dr. Seuss. Most of the words there don't make any sense and hardly mean anything in reality. However they provided the needed help to a person to remember the tale simply due to the rhyming effect.

Repetition

Repetition is the entire key to every memory exercise. Ensure to teach yourself to enact the actions every other time. For an instance, put your car keys inside the purse so that they are safe there. If you think your kids are late to school every day simply because they take time searching for their shoes or backpack, make them to learn to keep items in the allocated place every evening. Such minor memory tricks ascertain to keep your boss glad when you get to office everyday.

The Stress Of Alzheimer's

Alzheimer's disease has not found a cure yet and all that its sufferers would require is dedicated care and patience. It indeed is life threatening and can go a long way lacking a permanent cure. Alternative medicine including herbs and other dietary supplements is always sought after for help with respect to improving the condition. In spite of the alternative medicines, its effectiveness and safety is not much known. Another issue is regarding purity as the FDA shows no authority on supplement production. Reactions and few side effects go without any documentation and unnoticed in many cases. This then closes door to all further research. Most often consumers ignore the warning signs and in other cases warnings don't seem to be documented on the product. Quite many supplements would counteract with prescribed medications and can essentially increase more than few adverse reactions.

Disorder description

Recent studies have told that one out of ten elderly people suffer from Alzheimer's disease and by the year 2050, around 14 million people in the United States would perhaps be its victim. Alzheimer's disorder has seven stages with its duration of suffering varying from around three to about twenty years. In most cases this disorder is inherited. To some people, the disease is brought in due to irrational habits of smoking, drinking taking drugs etc, being clubbed by physical illness. This disorder, as termed to be one of the most complex of all has not reached a stage of permanent cure yet. People suffering from Alzheimer's disorder experience the pain for years as their sufferings are not just limited physically but emotionally and psychologically too. Consequently, they pass away within 6 years after the diagnosis. The patient's neurological system gets affected by the disease a lot before twenty or twenty five years. One of the worst endurance for these patients is dying in midst of unrecognizable people as they almost forget all their friends and family. The sufferers of this disorder trace their identity till they are totally consumed by its attributes.

Care takers

Alzheimer's disease makes it very difficult even for the care takers as they would apparently undergo a lot of stress financially, emotionally, and no doubt physically. All resources get utilized in its treatment which could prolong for years together without any hopes of total recovery. Care givers can make it more comfortable to release the stress by sticking names of pictures and other accessories so that the patients can know about it as they read the names. Tags could be stuck on drawers mentioning their content and also by placing a list of names with corresponding contact numbers especially of relatives, doctors etc, besides the telephone. This would help them in easier access. The caretakers can ensure that the patients are involved in their hobby activities so that they can reduce calls from them frequently. In later stages of Alzheimer's religious books could be always be read to the patients along with some soothing music. Proximity of family is one thing that would release the patient from all stress.

It is perhaps apparent that the care giver faces extreme stress all the while. Hence it is required that they are actively involved in community forums and other services. A number of emotions can harass the care taker which may include embarrassment, guilt, anger, grief and loneliness. Discussing and sharing feelings and incidents with peer care takers would release stress to quite an extent and ease the job. There is nothing more horrifying than seeing your dear one suffering and almost near to death. Quite often it becomes physically challenging too. Therefore in later stages one can seek help by hiring nurses or day care for the convenience of themselves and the patient as well.

Brain Food

Besides being a powerhouse of information repository, our brain keeps track of many other body functions. Some vital features of our brain include visual processing, motor control, auditory control, learning and sensation. Looking at all the functions and considerations you don't need to think twice about the brain being the most vital organ of your body. No matter what the malfunction of your brain is, it could be well understood when related to the new technology used in your computer.

Without the hard disk in your machine, your system is as efficient as being dead, as hard disk contains all significant information of your computer. If your computer hard disk is crashed, it is not possible for you to recover the lost data, at least most of it. All the same, if Alzheimer's disorder or Amnesia is struck, it at first destroys cells in our brain and memory gets affected. Memory failure makes us totally useless as we almost forget all skills we have learnt since a long period of time especially languages. Such diseases could turn man into things equivalent to a vegetable.

Every medication used to get back the memory is utilized for brain nourishment. Nourishment can be achieved through universal nourishment of brain and body. To have both brain and body to work together, we need to feed the body in right quantity and at the same time keep it active by taking part in mental and physical activities like memory games and jogging. Children, when in their initial stages, should explicitly be taken care of. Appropriate nutrition can make sure of their mental and physical well being.

From the initial stages of pregnancy, to-be mothers are advised with correct dosage of folic acid and multivitamins to assist in the growth of fetus, brain in specific. When dietary supplements and folic acid is low or not taken in right quantity, mental growth starts retarding. Initial growing stages of children, when they eat what they prefer and become choosy, health drinks are implied to be given to them.

One needs to take care of with dedication so that growth is not affected. Many health capsules have come to the market along with corresponding health drinks, however, the trusted and the best supplement is supposed to be cod-liver oil. Cod-liver oil is rich with Omega 3 fat helping in better faster growth of brain. Much research has proved that young children who are given cod liver oil almost on daily basis, manifest better memory and an active body.

We hardly make use of such natural supplements and over periods of time, drugs are interfered making things worse along with apparent everyday life stress. We are prone to various mental disorders including attention problems, confusion, foggy brain etc. One should ensure to remember that the core growth of the brain depends fully upon the nutrition given at an early age and the growth doesn't last a lifetime.

It needs to be supplemented on a customary basis. Over the counter, there are still many supplements available which are fortified with Folic Acid, Zinc, magnesium and other important nutrients for the brain. Any new supplements alone would not prove wonders over your brain unless you exercise well. Challenging memory very often by engaging in different mentally challenging activities and other memory games ensure right supply of oxygen and blood to the brain. Keeping blood pressure and cholesterol in control and taking good care of your heart help in cleansing arteries of blocks allowing better flow of blood. Estrogen level and other hormones should be maintained right as it directly affects the brain leading to several disorders in the longer run.

The Dangers Of Memory Loss

An important cause of losing memory is due to deprivation of sleep. You might have gone out to work or school in your in-house footwear just because your eyes were extra sleepy to change them. You might have even locked yourself outside home as you were very groggy due to lack of peaceful sleep, only too late to remember that your car and house keys were lying on the table in the kitchen. Have you been searching for your sunglasses every corner of your house, only to realize later that it is atop your forehead?

Quite many times memory loss looks funny to others. It would no doubt give you some silly stories producing giggles. Memory loss would serve to reveal forgotten incidents of other person's experience. Children too, can recall points of memory loss as a result of less sleep.

Resulting havoc

At times memory loss is quite dangerous and sometimes it could prove to be lethal and in some occasions losing memory is just very unfortunate. Deprived sleep would endure memory failure similar to a brain fog, going in a daze, not being able to focus, most often with a void expression. Notice a group of college students or teenagers after some trendy festive weekend. You would undoubtedly find someone in the group with head hanging with exhaustion with open mouths zoning out, or perhaps a void stare.

Furthermore, the worst of all cases of memory loss from lack of sleep is forgetting medicines which have already been taken once. You would end up taking the same thing again resulting in over dosage resulting in side effects, sometimes leading to hospitalization. If your lack of sleep takes you to a situation where you become sleepy to turn off the stove or burner, your house could catch perhaps catch fire with possibilities of injuring children or elderly in your care at home. If you are a young mother you would ignore the disturbances of your new born. Forgetting to change the baby's diapers could result in horrible rashes causing rawness and pain finally taking quite many days for its cure. When you get behind wheels of any vehicle in a drowsy state, you may not be alert to look both sides or may also forget the pedals on brake and gas momentarily, causing an unexpected accident.

After effects of medications

Medications can sometimes cause sleep disturbances resulting in loss of memory. On the other hand excessive medications too, make it not so easy to lay concentration. Forgetfulness in your job would possibly injure your co-worker or make you lose the job when you forget vital and generic things like meetings which ought to have been prepared for.

Apart from sleep deprivation, there could be other things which could lead to memory failure. However the fundamental thing is to seek a remedy for the trouble. Make sure that you take short naps whenever possible. Keep relaxing before bedtime instead of waiting to be on bed to relax. For new parents, chronic workaholics, or college students burning candles at both ends, it is required that they get adequate amount of rest and sleep, so as to avoid unfortunate events from sleep deprived memory failures. Ascertain to know that unless the mind and body are taken good care of, it would not continue to function right.

Herbs To Improve Your Memory

Improving one's memory with herbs does essentially sound bizarre. Using herbs for memory improvement has long been practiced not only in the United States of America, but also in many other countries. Egyptians, American Indians, Orientals and Greeks have all practiced the herb therapy for enhancing mind.

Various spicy food help in increasing cognitive functions of the brain. There are quite many spicy herbs available in the market.

Turmeric is one special spice usually used as an ingredient in several curry preparations. Curcumin is the precise ingredient within turmeric which helps in memory improvement. It helps in reducing disorders like Alzheimer's disease. Another herb is Ginger which contains Zingerrone that helps in defending the neurons in the brain resulting in memory improvement. Another spice, Cinnamon, boosts brain activity. Just by smelling Cinnamon, enhances your cognitive function by lifting up your mood. Each of these wonderful spices could be found at your local supermarket or grocery shop. It is present usually on or near the isle where basics of cooking ingredients like sugar and flour is usually kept.

United States is abundant of health food shops. Health food has become common among not just today's generation, but has also brought interest in adult shoppers. They suggest things such as ginkgo biloba as a good herb for improvement in blood flow to your brain. It is implied to have 80mg about three times a day.

Another famous herb increasing memory and guarding against senility, usually found in health shops is Gotu kola. This herb shows a calming effect. It is suggested to have half teaspoon in luke warm water about three times a day.

Siberian Ginseng could help your body to get adapted to stress helping to promote a strong and balanced nervous system. It also provides you with mild boost of energy. It is suggested to use about 250mg, two times every day.

It is always implied that you do your personal research before taking any of these herbs as they could at times make a negative interaction with certain medications you currently take. The idea of the herb in this context is mere improving of memory without any damage to your health in any way for that matter.

Herbs would not help in memory improvement by memory ingestion. Aromatherapy is one popular method to get your brain highly stimulated. Few herbs could be heated in water or sometimes like an ingredient in candle, or sometimes placed within a cloth over a potpourri burner with essential oils for inhaling. Aromatherapy is low cost addition for your steps glancing better mental health. It helps you relax, clears your mind, improves your mood and also sharpens your ability in focusing. Basil and Rosemary are two significant oils used in aromatherapy for memory improvement. Conversely, anything pleasant to one's nose helps in calming thoughts so that focusing gets clear and spirit is uplifted.

At the outset, a significant thing to take care of is considering to slow down your lifestyle and start to take good care of your body and mind. This is better, rather than suffering more after aging and taking the trouble of undoing the neglected effects. Remember to keep in mind that it is never late to carry a positive outlook and good charge.

Take Early Action To Retain Your Mental Health

The overall process of retaining recalling and storing information is referred to as memory. Most often we think about faring badly on our mental capability to remember things right. Furthermore, we seldom take this seriously in spite of recessing memory being one among several serious health disorders. Actions taken at a younger age could go a longer way in keeping our mental health right.

Experts have found out quite many methods to get over the disorders and improve the condition. Mnemonics is one such tool enhancing our capacity about remembering things based on relationship. Neurons in our brains receive or send signals. When the connections between the neurons are stronger, our memory gets better. As we practice various ways of strengthening the neurons, it goes longer way ensuring better and pacified memory. Memory generally degrades with mental disorders like stress and also with age. This is the reason why people need to get involved in leisure and fun activities so that the stress gets reduces to maximum. Various new experience and skills need to be implemented so that you move from routines functions. Trying new challenges and adventure ensure that your mind and body gets new environment to function well. Including brisk walk in daily exercising along with different cardiovascular exercises so that brain gets a good flow of blood and growth is enhanced. Brain could be stimulated by getting involved in puzzles, quizzes and brainstorming. Make sure to read several books and magazines staying updated with newspapers. Also ensure to retain good amount of information possible and keep recalling the same on daily basis by referring them in everyday conversation. You need to avoid medications like sleeping aids, anti depressants etc as they dull the human brain. One needs to kick off unhealthy habits of drinking, smoking and involvement in doping or drugs. Ensuring right amount of sleep, a minimum of eight hours a day would help the brain to stay alert and active.

Generally, memory can be short term or long term. Quite a few people boast about their memory as they can recall things as old as about twenty years or even more. There are others who forget even the past week's activity. These things typically depend upon the kind of attention paid. If you concentrate on the matter for eight seconds or more, the information gets stored right in the centre of your brain. Information retention is easily possible when you avoid multi tasking and undistracted attention. You can strengthen your memory by involving various senses and recalling the information to relate the data. You can also organize information in a much better way by referring it back as required, i.e., making use of appointment diaries or using address book. Breaking down significant complex substance into pieces and later interpreting, would also assist in boosting memory.

Diseases like cardiovascular diseases and diabetes also affect ones memory. Stress would also make it difficult to remember and concentrate on things. Healthy brain cells generation and memory restoration would be possible when you ensure to eat healthy. Legumes and green leafy veggies help in generating red blood cells take oxygen towards the brain. Beta-carotene and Vitamin B also improves oxygen flow within mind and body acting as antioxidants. Naturally healthy substances like these are present in vegetables and fruits such as sweet blue berries, tomato, potato, spinach, sweet potato, broccoli, citrus fruits, green tea, nuts and liver. Fresh water fishes like tuna and Salmon, Cod-liver oil, has Omega 3 fatty acids and are good for various cognitive functions. Vegetarian food like Flaxseed and walnut also has Omega 3 fatty acids. Folic acids and vitamin B deficiencies could be conquered by supplements available for the same. When these supplements are taken in right amount, it could boost heart functions helping in blood supply to brain and improving neuron functions for better pacified memory.

Various Ways To Improve Memory

So you keep forgetting the place where you have kept your spectacles every time these days? You try searching every nook and corner only to find it dangling over your forehead. These situations don't just make you a laughing stock but also question the state of mind. Such things when occur on everyday basis, would look and be disgusting to you and everyone around you. Quite many people have the memory loss syndrome and this typically depends upon the frequency of forgetfulness. The demanding lifestyle of today's era is so pressurizing that one hardly has time for oneself leading to slipping of important and generic information from the specified schedule. Adding to this, people's diet today does nothing to replenish the mind or body. Our unhealthy lifestyles without ample exercises have brought us to implement our robotic existence. Robots are mere computers and can work as they have been programmed, however the brain in humans would require right diets, healthy habits and proper exercise for better memory functioning.

Read below to know different ways of having memory improved.

Exercising is indispensible and should be done regularly to keep your body and mind attentive and active as every healthy body houses a healthy brain. You can also brush up your memory by actively taking part in different games and brain teasers to keep the brain alert. An easy memory game, "Memory" can be played with a deck of playing cards. This game can be played with as many as four people or less as playing all alone. All you need to do is spreading of cards evenly on the surface, and then lift a card to match the characters. When the characters don't match, keep the card from where it was taken and wait for a few chances till a match is appropriate remembering where the previous card was kept among all the other cards of the deck. Person matching more number of cards wins. If you prefer playing with words, try playing scrabble or any such word games which could actively challenge your memory by shaking up your vocabulary cache trove.

Many such games help to improve not just memory but also psychological functioning. Knowing new tactics and skills help in challenging the motor capacity of the brain. You can also join a language learning school for learning another language. Apart from this learning to play instruments could also get your brain more involving with ample mental exercise. More than anything, many computer games are being developed which could prove to be challenging and refreshing to your mind. The developing co ordination between hand and mind is very helpful for motor development. Yoga and exercise assists to keep a fresh mind by helping the concentration power being developed via meditation. This would help your body in two ways, i.e., by relaxing the body and structuring the alert system. The circulation of blood gets better helping to relax the brain improving its efficiency.

An equally significant substance of your physical well being for brain and body is relaxation. Any minor stress would lead to loss of memory and making it difficult for focusing. Quite many serious problems concerning stress call for physical test by doctors. These cases could lead to problems involving insomnia deteriorating mental health and making memorizing miserable.

People's busy schedule hardly allows them to keep in terms with their brain and body. This leads to destabilize various memory functions. The brain gets involved in several things at a time and just about concentrating on a single thing makes memory pace terrible. Therefore, in order to pacify memory we would initially need to change our lifestyles, indulging in better health practices which includes healthy eating and regular exercising.

Connecting Aging And Memory

It is a well-known fact that aging will affect memory for many different reasons. Family members, friends, spouses, and careers all suffer because of aging and memory loss. Loss of memory seems to be a part of life that may sneak up on a person, gradually growing worse until it is finally acknowledged as being serious to warrant attention.

One of the least-heard-of ways people are affected by loss of memory is called male menopause. It seems to be more of an issue to keep the health problems affecting men a secret than it is for women. The male pride can be extremely sensitive in the areas of failing health.

The first memory that seems to be affected by aging is short-term memory. It is easy to assume that one may be in the first stages of Alzheimer's when memory loss begins to occur. Indeed, some may laugh at the idea of male menopause. After all, everyone knows menopause is something women endure, right? Unfortunately, this is not at all true. Most men just never seek help for this condition because of not being aware of their feelings on a conscious level. Men are taught to put their emotions aside because to openly acknowledge them is perceived as a sign of weakness.

Forgetfulness is at the beginning of the list of changes occurring later in life. The mental processes are slowing down. We begin to run low on hormones after the age of 40.

There is a steroid hormone that the body will normally produce, using cholesterol as its main raw material. It converts into other steroids the body uses. The level of this hormone declines with age. Low doses such as 10-30 mg a day has been shown to be a memory enhancer with a punch! Possibly the most powerful memory enhancer of all, it is also an anti-inflammatory aid which helps arthritic conditions when given at high doses of 400-500 mg per day. Other benefits of this hormone are increased energy levels, balanced hormone levels, and repair to the sheath that covers neurons in the central nervous system.

Many women are able to laugh and joke with others about the effects of menopause, especially the memory loss. It may be harder to notice memory loss caused by menopause simply because women and men are both caught up in working and rearing their children. This causes preoccupation of the mind, due to the busy lifestyles.

Aging and memory loss are no joke, certainly, and even those who are able to find the humor in it may secretly be covering for the frustration it actually causes in their day-to-day lives. Forgetting can be a scary, intimidating part of the aging process. Once it becomes such a problem that the elderly are faced with their loss of independence, it is certainly no longer a joke to one of them. It can cause life-threatening confusion, sometimes causing them to wander away from home and get lost, cause a vehicle accident by wandering into the street, or subject them to the fierce elements of nature.

Improving Memory Using Mnemonic Tools

For those of you who may have never heard of the word, mnemonic means memory aid. It's an adjective related to things that help memory improvement. Teaching tools, if you will.

If you are a movie buff, you may have heard of the one called 'Johnny Mnemonic', a 1995 feature involving a data courier. Keanu Reeves is the star of the film. He carries a large data package, 320 gigabytes in size, in his mind. If he doesn't deliver it from Beijing to Newark, it will kill him. I suppose you could call this forced memory. It wasn't his brain that developed this computer chip, this memory tool. It contains a cure for a nerve syndrome of the future and puts his life in danger.

Some mnemonics would seem to be horrible techniques for the person who would prefer not to remember. However, this may be their only solution to overcoming a tragedy, in order to heal them. So, once more, forced memory is put into effect. The person must relive the mentally or emotionally damaging event to be able to move on with their lives and put the worst of the trauma behind them.

A coach, psychiatrist, hypnotist, counselor, pastor, trusted family member, teacher, or close friend may be needed to help give you moral support for the courage to use mnemonic tools.

Hypnosis has long been used as a mnemonic tool. Memory is a process of reconstruction rather than retrieval. Often the mind must be forced through hypnosis to reconstruct events that caused the person to suffer and attempt to protect themselves by choosing subconsciously to forget. Therefore, hypnosis may at times be a dangerous, however necessary, mnemonic tool.

Hypnosis is also a lucrative field. It is often used to help people stop an unhealthy habit, such as chronic nail-biting, smoking, overeating. It can also be used as a form of pain control. No matter how it is used, it involves the subconscious memory.

Mnemonic tools can be a positive way to overcome small annoyances. Suppose your short-term memory loss is disrupting your life in such a way that you are in a constant state of frustration. Small annoyances can add up to one big problem.

You may have subconsciously used mnemonic tools to learn to avoid certain disturbing memories. Like associating an object with someone who used that object to cause you pain. You decide to avoid use of that object to force yourself to leave the memory in the past. Maybe a dreaded uncle always wore purple, so to avoid having to constantly be reminded of the uncle, you decide to never buy an object the color purple. It may become a habit that you do without really thinking about it.

People have used flash cards, music, games, and repetition as mnemonics. Remember the old saying about tying a string around your finger to recall something important? Or placing a rubber band on your wrist, to pop whenever you are faced with a temptation you are trying to overcome?

Whatever the case may be, mnemonics can be very productive in memory improvement.

Research On Memory Loss

As the threat of memory based diseases such as Amnesia and Alzheimer is increasing, the medical fraternity is trying their best to come out with the best of solution. Several researches are being carried on globally to make difference to such conditions. Some achievement has been made so far but nothing considerable as come so far. As Alzheimer is being a constant threat to the growing number of elderlies according to one of the statistics nearly 65% of them are exposed to the disease. Little diagnosis could be made so far as not too many are aware of the condition and refer it to the aging process.

Until they realize that it's affecting their quality of life. So much so that it has damaging effect on them in various ways such as psychological, emotional and financial. Especially in a nuclear family setup older folks find themselves ignored most of the time. Due to ignorance and little awareness the disease is barely diagnosed on time and leads to death.

Current research on memory loss reveals that Omega 3 fats are helpful in declining such conditions. Folic acid and folate are also known to help the condition; supplements if taken for 3 years can significantly help on improving cognitive functions. People who consume fish on a regular basis have lesser chances of suffering from any form of Dementia. Vegetables also are known to be rich in few minerals and vitamin that helps in neurons functions. Exercise is however the most important way to keep the brain active as it leads to better blood circulating throughout body and brain.

According to a study those who exercise three times a week are less prone to develop disease such as Alzheimer. Brain diet mostly constitutes of low saturated fats, coniferous vegetables, fruit and fish with omega-3 fatty acids. An active social life enhances our defenses and builds immunity and reduces inflammation. Green tea also may work as wonder for the brain research has proved that those who have regular intake of green tea are less likely to suffer from cognitive impairment.

Drinking 2 servings of green tea a day can help keep any cognitive dysfunction at bay. Keeping a check on weight also helps to counter Dementia. Blood pressure and cholesterol control can lower the risk of Alzheimer. Eating leafy green vegetables and coniferous veggies also helps in restoring cognitive functions. So one should carefully include all the green vegetables such as broccoli and spinach in one's diet plan.

Older people who exercise on a regular basis are known to generate more brain cells than their counterparts who do not exercise and also learn new skills more effectively. Consuming fruits and veggies rich in antioxidants helps in boosting metabolism and maintain the integrity of nerve cell components. Magnesium and Zinc intake are also known to improve and maintain brain receptors thus enhancing memory.

Research has also proven blueberries, Ginseng, Gastrodine and Gingko Biloba to help create new neurons and improve memory functions. Vitamin B12, vitamin C, vitamin E and other nutritional supplements intake helps restoring memory function and build new cells However justifiable amount of caffeine taken thru tea and coffee also sharpens brain proven by a recent research. Lowering of cortisol level and stress can help regenerate its power to remember and learn. Aerobics can protect brain tissue from aging and decline. These are results of few researches that have been done to check memory loss and brain related disorder.

To Improve What? Oh Yes, Memory!

How many times have you had the exact word you needed on the tip of your tongue only to have it tease and evade your memory? Who hasn't written a list to remember and then forgotten the list! Or perhaps you asked someone to help you remember and they forgot. Maybe you hid something from yourself in a special place you were sure to recall and spent weeks searching for the item because you forgot where you hid it. How many Easter eggs have been hidden, only to rot several days later because the person who hid the eggs forgot where they put them? What about that person you spent weeks secretly adoring, finally got the perfect chance to make their acquaintance, and then suffered a mental freeze?

Was a bill paid late because you forgot to make a note on your calendar, notes you try to remember to transfer from each month previous? Did you forget someone's birthday, someone like your child or parent or, Heaven forbid, your spouse? Did you forget to feed your dog, and then get angry because he's persistently trying to get your attention while you're busy with an important call? Was that you who were asked by your loving wife or husband to bring a drink on a hot day of yard work, while your loved one tolls away with their chores as you relax in the air conditioning? Oops! Sorry, honey. By the way, that silly doctor's office called, you missed your appointment you were adamant they squeeze into their busy schedule. Oh, dear, was that today?

Sometimes it seems that no matter what we do to try to jog our memories, they betray us at the worst possible moments. Children are forgotten at school, standing in the car pick-up line. The groceries are left to ruin in the back seat of the car because the phone rang just as you opened the front door. A bag is left at the store holding something you bought that shows on your receipt, but got lost because of the many bags you had to maneuver into the buggy while holding the crying baby. A cup is balanced on top of a vehicle, only to topple off as the driver pulls away.

Every day people somewhere complain about memory loss, mostly temporary and short-term memory loss. Many times it is simply a result of preoccupation and jammed, hectic schedules. Sometimes it is from lack of sleep due to illness of one's self or one's child, or a night spent in a hospital by a loved one's side.

Proper rest and relaxation are important for normal mental function. Harried families often neglect to even allow themselves relief on a vacation, often times returning more tired and mentally stressed than before their trip. Yet, the solution can be so simple as to be overlooked. What is the answer? Take care of yourself. Learn how much is too much and start saying no, whether to yourself or to someone needing just a tiny little favor that throws your whole schedule out of whack when you are already stressed enough.

Boost Your Memory

As we age we often find that certain parts of our bodies aren't working as well as they once did. One of the most common complaints is in the area of memory. Many people suffer memory loss, or a clouded memory. They can pinpoint major events of their lives but when it comes to the finer details they can't quite put their finger on every point.

This isn't an issue that just affects the elderly. Memory loss can happen to anyone of any age. Life is busy and when we have so much on our minds, some information might slip between the cracks, leaving us frustrated that we aren't as clear-minded as we once were. It can be something as simple as forgetting where we last put the car keys or when a friend's birthday is. If it happens occasionally we may overlook it as just having too much on our minds and therefore it becomes harder to retain all the information we need to. However if it's an ongoing problem it is something we need to address.

Memory loss can be an embarrassing issue and many people hesitate to talk about it with family, with friends and even with their physician. They view it as a sign of aging and because they may not be ready to face being older, they ignore the problem. They assume that it happens to everyone and they just accept it.

There are solutions to the problem of memory loss. Depending on the seriousness of the problem, the remedies can range from exercises to enhance your memory, to natural supplements that help clear the mind or in some cases to traditional prescription medications.

Another approach that works for many people is to use aids in helping them remember important dates or events. Having a method of keeping track of things that involves writing them down when they are fresh in the mind guarantees that you won't forget them, because you can refer back to them. It also serves another purpose, often when we write things down we can visualize the note later. Our mind will pull it back up and before we even refer to the notebook or day planner, we have recalled the name, date or event.

Some people have found it helpful to repeat things out loud. This works to reinforce the information and implant it into the memory. This seems to work especially well for people who have trouble remembering names when they are meeting someone for the first time.

Memory loss is a condition that can affect anyone. By taking a few small steps you can work towards building your memory back up. It's much like the Memory Game that children play when they are small to exercise that part of their mind. The adult version may differ a bit, but the principle is very much the same. Exercising the mind is much like exercising any muscle within your body. If it's not stimulated our memory won't work as well as it once did.

Meditation And Memory

Meditation is a wonderful method of helping the entire body to relax. Through a system of breathing exercises the body naturally feels the stress being released and for many people it allows them to be much more open and receptive.

Meditation can also aid in helping with memory. When a person feels relaxed the memory seems to function much better. Through the use of breathing and concentration the memory feels alive and vibrant once again.

Remember the last time you forgot someone's name or their birthday? It was probably during a period where you had a great deal on your mind or you were feeling stress. Upon realizing your forgetfulness this generally stirs up even more anxiety which again leads to more memory problems. It's a cycle that some people find themselves constantly in.

By employing some of the techniques of meditation that people have been using for years, you can help open up your mind and memory thus allowing it to function better. It's wonderful to imagine having the ability to recall names, numbers and important dates without having to look for pieces of paper or check a calendar. Instead it would all be there within your memory.

Meditation does not need to be a complicated process. There are simple exercises that anyone can do for a few moments each day that will help boost the memory. The key to using meditation as a memory booster is that it will help build concentration which works hand in hand with developing memory.

Finding a quiet spot is very helpful when you want to meditate. Some people also feel that having essential oils or candles burning adds to the necessary ambiance. If that does help you relax than it's going to beneficial to the entire process including helping you to reenergize your mind. There are also certain scents of oils and candles that are said to be beneficial for memory function.

Meditation can be taught in a class and there are usually classes offered at natural health care facilities and often even at regular gyms. Some of the classes are geared towards helping the memory to function. For a person who feels as though their mind isn't as sharp as it once was, taking one of these classes will benefit them for years to come. Building up a regular routine of meditation to aid in boosting the memory will also build self-esteem. Feeling as though you are on top of your game mentally is a wonderful self-image booster.

For someone who feels less comfortable within a class of people learning meditation, there are many books and manuals that offer substantial information on mediation as a method of empowering the memory. Some offer illustrations of body position and along with descriptions for the breathing exercises. Following the methods outlined daily will open the person up to the benefits of meditation. By using the techniques described they will not only be relaxing their bodies but fueling their memory as well. Having a relaxed and clear mind is one of the most important aspects to having a strong memory.

Boost Your Memory With Caffeine

There have been a lot of negative reviews of the consequences of consuming coffee, tea or eating chocolate because of the amount of caffeine that these substances contain. There might be a silver lining to the caffeine cloud though and that's how caffeine can play an important role in boosting your memory.

Often we experience short term memory problems. At times it can be whether we turned off the water after we brushed our teeth or if we locked the door before we went to bed. These things can nag at our minds enough that we turn our car around to make certain that we won't be faced with a flood because of running water or we jump out of bed only to find that we did indeed lock the door.

Life is busy and it's easy to forget some of the smaller things that we take for granted. Our minds might have trouble focusing because of a conflict at work or stress at home. This isn't an uncommon occurrence and it happens everyday to people of every age. Losing track of tiny details is common but certainly not something that we need to live with. There are steps that we can take to improve our memory enough that we never have to deal with having our minds filled with those nagging thoughts again.

If you find that you're one of the people who can't put their finger on certain small facts and it has become a frustration for you, it might be time to consider the benefit of caffeine in relation to short term memory.

Caffeine is a stimulant and it works to stimulate not only our hearts but our minds as well. It can give a person the extra boost they need to clear their mind. Many people feel the need to have a cup of coffee each morning so they can focus. The caffeine that is found within the coffee jolts the brain and the memory can retain more information. You probably know someone who says that they can't function until they've had their coffee. It appears that there's more truth in that statement than most of us have ever realized. That first cup of morning coffee gets the memory gears moving in many people.

This can be especially important for many people at work. Having the ability to retain important information is essential for their employment. If they find their memory lacking it could have serious consequences that stretch far beyond some of the minor annoyances that they might experience at home when they forget to do things.

A cup of coffee or tea in the morning might be just the prescription to boost the memory enough that the rest of the day you function at full memory capacity. The same can be said for the lull that many people experience by mid-afternoon. Having a piece of chocolate or a cup of hot chocolate stimulates your memory again and the rest of the day will flow as smoothly as the beginning did.

What To Eat To Boost Your Memory

Being aware of the nutritional value of the foods we eat is obviously essential to a healthy body. Eating the right combination of carbohydrates, proteins and healthy fats works towards keeping muscles strong and organs functioning the way nature intended.

Our minds are no different and eating foods rich in certain nutrients can help alleviate brain fog and boost our memories back to the place they were when we were younger. It only seems natural that since most of our body is fueled by the healthiest of foods, feeding our minds the same way follows suit.

There has been extensive research done into studying the effects of certain minerals and vitamins in relation to brain function. It's common sense that sugar although a temporary stimulant quickly loses it's luster and although we might feel very vibrant and alive after eating a candy bar, within an hour or two our bodies have become sluggish and less responsive. Our minds and therefore our memories would feel the same high and crashing low if fed a diet of sweets.

Eating sensible is important for boosting your memory. Foods that are rich in antioxidants are said to work in helping memory function. The benefits of antioxidants are often associated with fighting cancer and playing a positive role in certain diseases of the heart. Now with the knowledge that they also work towards improved memory function, having them as a staple in the daily diet seems natural. Some examples of foods readily available that are high in antioxidants include carrots and certain kinds of nuts. Green tea is also an excellent source of antioxidants and its benefits reach well beyond boosting the memory.

Another product that helps with memory function is soy. Eating foods like tofu will provide benefits that help improve memory. Another great source of soy is the soy milks that are available in most food markets. Many are flavored and the taste although not exactly the same as cow's milk is considered appealing to many people. Soy also offers many other benefits to the body and knowing that it can help with boosting your memory is good stimulation for trying it and possibly making it a regular part of your diet.

Most people use oil in some form for cooking and if choosing a specific type of oil can boost your memory it would seem sensible to incorporate it into your everyday cooking. Olive oil is a healthy choice for many reasons including its effects on memory function. Using it to cook or within salad dressing is a healthy way to work towards having less brain cloudiness and improved memory clarity. It's another step towards feeling confident that you are doing everything you can to ensure that your memory stays sharp.

Adjusting one's diet to balance the effects of memory loss seems a perfect solution. With just a small change in the consumption of certain foods anyone can feel as though they are not only eating healthier but also improving their memory.

Natural Remedies That Work To Boost Your Memory

Natural supplements are gaining popularity as they work towards improving many aspects of health and well-being. There are supplements available that aid in memory clarity and have a positive effect on boosting memory. These remedies are derived from substances that occur naturally and have been consumed in one form or another for centuries. Their impact on body functions proven over time and their ability to aid in clearing a cloudy memory are worth investigating.

A bit of research will reveal one supplement that seems to lead the pack when it comes to keeping a person's ability to remember at its highest level. That supplement is Gingko Biloba Extract. The reason that it's thought to have such a significant impact on memory function is that it helps with the flow of blood throughout the body. This of course includes the flow of blood to the brain. Blood contains oxygen and having a steady and constant flow of blood keeps the memory sharp. There are numerous different brand names of supplements that proclaim to be the best source of Gingko Biloba Extract therefore it's up the potential consumer to decide which one is best suited for their needs.

Another supplement that appears to offer benefits in the memory department is rosemary. Rosemary is often thought of as a spice we use when cooking. The effects of it as a herbal supplement are interesting. Rosemary works as a way of stimulating the brain. Keeping the brain stimulated is essential in making certain that memory is working correctly. There are different varieties of supplements that contain rosemary and checking the dosage and strength is always recommended.

Many of the natural remedies that offer benefits in memory function work towards other health goals as well. An example of this is green tea. Green tea is becoming a natural cure for many ailments or conditions. It's thought to have a positive effect on memory function and along with black tea when consumed in moderation seems to help in optimizing a person's ability to remember.

Ginseng also seems related to improved memory function. Ginseng is a herb that is often associated with improving energy and people who are aging swear by its ability to revitalize. If it has this profound effect on other parts of the body it would seem reasonable that it would work as a booster to the mind and the memory. There are several different supplements that can be purchased that contain ginseng and it's important to weight the benefits of the other ingredients when choosing one that is specifically formulated in helping with memory function.

For people who are just beginning to feel the signs of memory loss, possibly because of age or in some cases with the stress of everyday life small details seem to slip the mind, taking a natural supplement can be the ideal solution. They generally offer fewer side effects than traditional medication along with substantial benefits that reach well beyond their memory boosting attributes.

Boosting Your Memory During Menopause

As women age their bodies inevitably change. After decades of maturing and living, women find themselves entering menopause. With the end of menstruation, many women experience numerous side effects. Many are nothing more than inconvenience, the dreaded cold and hot spells and the hair loss. However for many women menopause also brings about memory loss and a feeling of forgetfulness. Small details that they once retained with ease now elude them.

This is now the time that many women want to experience the same clarity they had years ago. Finding a way to boost their memory is one way they can control the changes their body is going through. Dealing with daily brain fog is a problem that can be addressed.

An often thought cause of declining memory function in women of menopause age is a lower level of estrogen in the body. As the body nears menopause and prepares to cease monthly menstruation, the estrogen levels that were once strong begin to decline. Many women turn towards conventional medicine that speaks to the benefits of taking an estrogen supplement as a means to ward off the loss of memory that plagues women entering menopause.

They are prescribed a daily or weekly dose of estrogen which is designed to replace the estrogen lost through the process of aging. The body absorbs the added supplements and the mind becomes focused and clear again as it was when the woman was younger. The estrogen acting as a booster for the memory this results in the fogginess that was being felt to disappear.

One of the best defenses against a loss of memory for maturing women is exercise. This not only works as a strong stimulant for the brain but it helps to clear the mind. Often when a person is thinking of too many things at once, the brain becomes almost overloaded and just as a cup or bowl becomes full and the liquid seeps out over the edge, so do some details in a memory that is filled to capacity. Menopause often brings about sadness or bouts of depression in women.

As women enter a new stage in life they remember their younger years and the promise that those years had. Now looking back they might recall many of the things they didn't accomplish. This can lead to a feeling of sadness or depression which also contributes to reduced memory. By exercising in a moderate way daily or even several times a week, the body responds to that stimulation by helping to relieve the sense of depression, thus working towards feeling as though the memory is back on target.

Being mentally stimulated also helps the menopausal women in many ways. Be it reading a book to their grandchild or playing a friendly game of cards, they are engaging their memories. By keeping focused on using their minds, their memory naturally stays alert. Boosting the memory this way is a great method of keeping the menopausal women as aware as she was decades ago.

Even though the menopausal woman has to accept the many changes that her body is going through, she doesn't have to accept memory changes at all. Boosting her memory is a vitally important step to keeping herself young.

Boost Your Child's Memory

Every parent wants their child to flourish and succeed. As they begin school many mothers and fathers help their children to memorize and recite the alphabet and to learn the sounds that the letters make. These are the beginning memory skills that all children need.

An early method of introducing your child to memory exercises is the games that involve matching pictures or words. A game like this can be purchased very inexpensively and usually entails several small cards with simple pictures on them that children turn over after viewing, remembering where certain images are helps them score points. Even children as small as three or four-years-old can take part and this is a wonderful method of not only boosting their memory, but it gives parents a fantastic opportunity to interact with their child.

As children mature they begin to read. Reading involves not only sounding out the letters, joining them together into words, but many words are simply remembered. Children become familiar with the pattern of letters and the word becomes embedded in their minds. The same method occurs when children learn to count from one to ten. After reciting the numbers over and over again, their memory takes hold and they are able to count, first from one to five and then higher and higher.

Another great technique for both moms and dads to help their toddlers remember things is to incorporate memory building exercises into everyday activities. This could involve time spent walking outside or playing at the park. Pointing to items such as a tree, a flower or a dog and having the child repeat the word. This helps build up their memory and if it's repeated over and over again, before long the child will blurt out the word from memory when they spot the item.

Television is often a highly debated subject when it comes to its influence on children. However, there are some programs that if a toddler watches while in the company of a parent or care-giver can become fuel for the memory. These types of programs actually make great learning tools. If a child hears a song daily, eventually they will remember the words and chime in, singing along. Even young children can hold this type of information - the lyrics and the tune - in their memories. Depending on the type of programs that you choose for your child, they might boost his or her memory which helps to ready them for when they enter school. Stimulating the brain can start at any age.

Helping children work on the muscle of their memory doesn't stop when they learn to read and write. Often, older children struggle with tests or exams finding it hard to retain all the necessary information. There are steps that a parent can take to aid their older children in readying for examinations. A great method is to encourage the child to read over their notes out loud. Often when we hear information as opposed to just reading it, our memory absorbs it much quicker. Having your child read his or her notes to you and then using that information to quiz them on important points will work towards implanting the information in their memory.

Boost Your Memory To Remember People's Names

Almost everyone has been in a situation where someone's name slips your mind. You have been introduced to them in the past but trying to remember their name is futile. Instead you fumble along, looking for them to hand you a clue. This is an embarrassing situation for not only the person whose memory seems to have taken a mini-vacation, but it's also difficult for the person whose name you forgot. It might make them feel slighted or unimportant.

There are tricks that the average person can employ that will help will boosting the memory and aiding in remembering important things including names. One technique that many people swear by is saying the name out loud once the person has introduced themselves to you. By repeating it you are hearing it again and the name becomes associated in your memory with the person's face.

You might also try asking them pointed questions while using their names. For instance, looking directly at them while saying, "What do you do for a living, Lisa?" Or "Do you have any children, Paul?" Again the idea is to use the name in a way that you are hearing it giving your memory an additional opportunity to absorb it.

Studying the person's face and hair when you are first introduced to them can work as well. Most people have something different about them, be it a mole or perhaps a tooth that is slightly askew. If you concentrate on that aspect and then associate it with their name, your memory will bind the two together. For instance, if you are introduced to a woman named Anne who has a mole above her left eye it would be wise to focus on that as you repeat her name silently. Your memory will connect the two and then if you happen to see Anne again the mole above her eye will be the catalyst that jogs you into remembering her name.

If you are faced with a large group of people whose names are all new to you, both of these techniques might prove handy. Most people will not expect someone to recall their names if they are part of a huge crowd. All we need to do is remember back to grade school when the teacher would place the students in rows according to a seating plan.

It is almost impossible for any teacher to memorize twenty-five or thirty names within the first few days of school, so having the seating plan affords the teacher the ability to glance at the name that's noted on the plan and associate it with the child's face. As adults we don't have the luxury of a seating plan when we meet people in a business or social setting so it's important to find a technique that gives your memory a boost. If you do that, the next time you come face-to-face with someone you've already been introduced to, you'll remember their name.

Exercise Your Way To A Better Memory

Exercise is fundamental in maintaining a healthy body. Activities that stimulate the body aid in many areas including keeping our muscles toned, and also in reducing weight. Another substantial benefit to regular physical exercise is that it appears that it aids in boosting the memory.

When we exercise our heart beats at a faster rate. When our hearts beat faster the blood within our bodies flows at a quicker pace. This translates into more blood moving through the brain. This equals improvement in certain brain functions including memory. That means that by exercising we are improving our skills to remember many things. Often as we age in particular we become a bit forgetful and naturally associate that as a normal part of getting older. However, the same exercise that you do to improve how you feel, can also improve your ability to retain information. That's an incredible bonus.

The type of exercise doesn't appear to be as important as the duration. Getting your heart up to a certain pace and keeping it there for a specific time is essential. Therefore it's wise to choose an activity that you enjoy. Doing something pleasurable helps the time pass quickly and before you know it your memory will have the work-out it needs to stay on track.

Walking outdoors is an inexpensive way to exercise not only your body but your memory as well. A twenty or thirty minute walk several times a week will aid in boosting your memory. It would also be wise to engage in mental exercises as you are walking. Testing yourself on the names of the streets that you regularly pass, becomes a silent game of memory. Once you have the street names mastered you can shift your focus to other elements, perhaps house numbers or colors of the homes. This is a wonderful way to boost your memory in more ways than one all at the same time.

Another relaxing and gentle form of exercise is swimming. Many people enjoy daily swims throughout the entire year. Getting the blood flowing helps in memory function as well as toning the body. Most indoor swimming pools also offer swimming classes that involve aerobics. This is a great method of partaking in exercise. The instructor demonstrates several sequences of moves that the participants mimic. This also is a great memory game. The repetition of the exercises helps embed them in the memory. Soon the swimmer is recalling the moves straight from memory.

Going to a gym is also a great way to work the entire body. There are many pieces of equipment that can be used to increase heart rate and blood flow to the brain. There are also other ways to get a boost to your memory through physical activity that isn't traditionally thought of as exercise. One such method is dancing. By putting on some favorite music, moving the furniture and taking a spin around the floor, your memory is getting the exercise it craves. Movement is essential to memory!

Vitamin B - The Miracle Memory Supplement?

Taking a multi-vitamin everyday is a great way to supplement one's diet. The various vitamins and minerals supplied add fuel to a healthy body. Some of those vitamins may play an even more important role when it comes to memory.

There have been studies that suggest that if a person has lower levels of some of the B Vitamins that they may be more prone to developing Alzheimer's disease. This is a frightening prospect for most people. The idea of slowly losing the ability to remember small details until it progresses into the inability to remember anything at all. Tests conducted on some individuals who do suffer from Alzheimer's have shown a lack of the B Vitamins in their bodies. Therefore using that knowledge to improve the intake and absorption of the vitamin might slow down the progress of the memory loss and the onset of the ravages of the disease.

Taking a supplement rich in B Vitamins is one approach. There are several supplements available that a person can take daily to boost their Vitamin B intake resulting in a boost to their memory. It's best to consult with a health care professional who is familiar with the effects of Vitamin B on memory. They have the knowledge necessary to recommend a supplement that will provide the memory boosting benefits that the patient most needs.

However, taking a pill isn't the only way to get more Vitamin B into your body. There are certain foods that are rich in B Vitamins and offer the opportunity to boost your memory function in the most natural way. If this is the approach then it's as simple as incorporating specific foods into the diet that work towards building the memory.

Liver is a very good source of Vitamin B but many people have difficulty eating liver. For those that do enjoy it, it provides a nutritious and easy method of helping combat the effects of memory loss with aging. Salmon is another food that is rich in Vitamin B. With all the easy and delicious methods of preparing salmon it can become a staple in anyone's diet.

Developing a common sense approach to using Vitamin B as a supplement to aid in memory function is relatively easy. Depending on your tastes, if the foods rich in Vitamin B aren't appealing, visiting your physician or a health food store and inquiring about a supplement is a wise decision. Although it's not common for individuals to lack Vitamin B within their bodies, it does happen. In fact it occurs more readily in elderly people which might account for the reason behind their feelings of forgetfulness. By asking their physicians about the value of a supplement they might just be taking the first step to a renewed memory.

It can be disheartening to forget small details such as names or birthdays. Having the ability to regain some of the confidence that comes with a strong memory is a way to renew your outlook. Vitamin B is a safe and efficient way to do that.

How Do Science And Memory Connect?

One way science and memory connect is through the side effects of a medication that may cause memory loss. Another way is through trying to improve memory.

Take Alzheimer's for example. It is now a well recognized disease that has been under much scientific study. In this disease, memory loss begins when the entorhinal cortex, an area of brain involved in building new memories, loses neurons faster then they are being replaced. The human brain was once thought to have all the brain cells possible at birth. Now science has uncovered the fact that human and primate brains can generate new nerve cells (neurons) after birth.

These nerve cells are made in the cerebral cortex throughout the life span. The number of neurons stays fairly constant, but the ones lost in each area are replaced anew. If the production of new ones can't keep up with those dying or being removed, the brain function begins to decline. Science has found that when the number is reduced by one-third, the short term memory begins to fail, hence Alzheimer's.

It is thought that certain antioxidants have the ability to significantly delay the effects of Alzheimer's. In people under the age of 80, the chance of developing this disease could be reduced by 50 percent by taking low doses (200 to 400 mg) of ibuprofen for two or more years. There are also certain activity programs that can delay the progression of the disease. Scientists believe the progression can be delayed by regular exercise.

Lifestyle behaviors must be altered to age in a healthy way. This healthy aging includes retaining healthy memory function. The way one eats, sleeps, drinks, smokes, lacks adequate physical and mental exercise, and allows an overabundance of stress on a regular, long-lasting basis all affect good health.

Illegal use of drugs has long been known to affect memory function. It kills brain cells, as does the long-term overuse of alcohol. Two prescription drugs that have had memory loss as side effects are Prozac and Zoloft. The patients' symptoms would improve as far as the reason they were put on these drugs, but once memory loss began to develop, the patients would have to be taken off them.

The process of knowing and perceiving is called cognition. Alzheimer's and disorders related to it all have one thing in common: cognitive impairment. As long as only one symptom exists, the diseases are distinct from each other. If not treated early enough and effectively, other brain areas begin to be affected and the symptoms make it hard to diagnose which disease is present.

One disease similar to Alzheimer's disease is dementia. There are different types of dementia. There is Parkinson's Dementia, Frontal-Temporal Lobe Dementia, Vascular Dementia, Subcortical Vascular Dementia, dementia due to head injury, and dementia from cancer and cancer treatment.

One thing is certain, regardless of your reason for memory loss, science and advanced technology are making it easier every day to single out and treat the problem.

How To Memorize

To memorize is to store information in your brain for reuse later. The definition of memory is the power or act of remembering. The definition of remembering is to recall, to bring back to mind by an effort.

Some people are able to memorize things temporarily and then forget them when they are no longer of use. Many times this is the case with a person who may study just for the sake of passing a test containing information they don't feel is of particular importance, yet they are required to know it anyway for a job or to pass to the next level of a class or school. Preschoolers must make the effort to memorize the alphabet, to recognize colors, to write their names. This type of information is of importance in their daily lives as they go through each year of school. Often an older child will have to memorize the multiplication tables or all the states in the United States.

Use of flash cards is a well-known way to memorize. If you are studying a foreign language, you can use the flash cards to write one interpretation on one side, and the other version of the word on the other side. Children's books often use the flash method to tell a story that will help the child memorize. Pop-ups are a fun way to learn. Many books will use pictures of animals, toys, or even food to help the child memorize the name of a word and its proper usage.

Have you ever taught tricks to a dog? It must memorize the steps to the trick in the process of learning what you want. Teaching a parrot to talk requires the parrot to memorize the words you choose for it to learn. Sometimes an animal can memorize the path home or a smell of certain people. Maybe you need to learn some tricks, like recalling names at a party!
To remember combinations, middle school students must memorize the numbers that will open their locks. They also have to memorize their school ID numbers to go through the line in the cafeteria for billing to their lunch accounts.

Sometimes people have to make phone calls and don't have pen and paper ready. They may have to temporarily memorize the number given them by an operator assistant.

If you have children, you may have asked them to memorize things like their phone numbers and addresses in case they get lost. Their teachers may even require this at the beginning of their school year in the younger grades of education.

There are a vast number of books written on the process to improve memory. Word games were invented for such a use. Even crossword puzzles require extensive use of the memory. Studies have been done for years on ways to trick your mind to memorize. Playing with people's names can help you memorize them.

Make a rhyming game in your mind with the name. Rhyming stories are a fun way to memorize. Or you could try associating the name with a color. Whatever your choice to improve your memory, it can only benefit you to succeed!

Memory And Your Health

Want an enviable memory? Start leading a healthy life fused with exercises that boosts blood circulation to that area of brain that is responsible for memory. A sedentary lifestyle causes not only a lethargic body but also a diminishing static brain. While you take a jog make sure that that the exercise regimen also includes cardio vascular exercises. A lapse is memory can often be an indication of start of Alzheimer disease especially in elderlies.

With growing awareness of the disease it is more probable that people suspect disease the moment they identify a small gap in memory. It mostly occurs at the age of 50 or more with ageing and diminishing nutrition. A lot also depend on the stress level for memory to deteriorate before time. However, it is perfectly normal to forget a thing or two at later stage in life. Besides stress, people deprived of sleep specially those working odd hours are prone to memory loss. Only a well-rested body and brain can perform well.

There are many over the counter drugs apart from herbal medication to boost memory. Few people believe that taking Gingko Biloba helps in restoring memory others rely on memory formula enriched with vitamin and minerals. These herbs and medication expand blood vessels, fight free radicals, boost immune system and decreases the level of depression and stress.

Other naturally occurring substance that helps in ensuring proper blood circulation to brain are rosemary, ginseng and green tea. Green tea contains plethora of benefits that surpasses any her from improving blood circulation to weight maintenance. Their antioxidant helps fight cancer and promotes healing. It is used across skin preparations as it acts as soother and healer. It is also known for its anti-aging benefits. Other medication promises to increase the concentration level and boost brainpower by improving oxygen flow to the brain.

While aging people might want to indulge in the above-mentioned supplements and medication the younger lot can always look for memory building games online or otherwise. There are memory plans on internet such as pmemory.com, Brain age, Big brain academy that promises to build a phenomenal memory. But the first and foremost step toward acquiring a great memory is to squash the laziness syndrome and start feeling active. But surf to these online memory shacks are certainly not as good as visiting your local farmer market and grabbing a broccoli instead. These powerful veggies are sure to get the cognitive clock ticking. According to latest research studies broccoli, cauliflowers and other Cruciferous vegetables improves the memory and reverse the aging process by nothing less than one and half year. Spinach that is high on folate is proved to reduce the risk of Alzheimer by breaking the homocysteine, an amino acid that is toxic to the nerve cell. Usage of unsaturated or hydrogenated fats have also proved to reduce the risk of Alzheimer and memory loss.

However there are other reasons that can be attributed to memory loss called Amnesia its is a symptom that causes complete memory blackout generally caused by head injury, drug toxicity, stroke, paralysis attack, emotional shock, and infection. These memories can be recovered through psychotherapy but it few cases it is observed that the condition prevails for lifetime resulting in subject to live a completely new life.

Recover Diminishing Memory

There are various ways to recover diminishing memory. Few aids have been discovered to assist them entire procedure such as Memory Lifter it helps in memorizing vocabulary or language. Hormonal therapy is used in women to help their retarding memory due to menopausal hormonal change in the body. It has proved the hormonal therapy has direct and immediate on the critical part of brain that controls memory functions.

It also lowers the risk of Alzheimer in women. However more research is going into this study and few experts have criticized this therapy. But critics have also criticized Mnemonics and mention that this technique is not 100 accurate actually no technique is 100% fool proof as there is always room for one to forget and Mnemonics and its dynamics are complicated for people who are unaware of Esperanto grammar besides it also carry some costs. There is also this myth that with age memory deteriorates but it's not true for all as few people are less prone to memory loss and Alzheimer because a well trained mind is stronger than other system of our body and though it does loses some neurons due to ageing but a lot depends on training and knowledge. Popping pills are considered to be a solution by many but the supplements just makes our body healthier and thus automatically affecting the activeness of our brain hence no memory pill is a magic pill to boost memory. But still there are many who believe in consuming memory food to enhance their memory. Though taking regular vitamins and minerals are good for health and body but excess of anything is harmful and it goes for the herb Ginkgo Biloba too.

If eaten to excess it can cause bleeding in the brain. Hence the most reliable treatment is consumption of green fruits and antioxidants rich fruits and vegetables. Monitoring depression and anxiety helps in recovering from memory loss besides a relaxed brain and body gets the mind in an active frame. Iron is also a stimulator of neuron transmitter that helps in functioning of memory properly.

In long run our brain is impaired and memory is affected by the usage of drug as the chemicals reacts with our body the neurons are inflicted and lost. Nicotine and alcohol have been proved to cause memory loss. Smoking and drinking can cause stroke or other heart ailments that interfere with the flow of neuron to our body causing memory loss. Stimulants like tea and coffee are good in adequate quantity as they keep us alert when we want to without causing neurotic damage. Memory loss can also happen if an information or knowledge has not been used for a considerable amount of time it becomes susceptible to be lost or needs brushing up. One can also improve their memory by the usage of memory optimizer. A process that uses the memory effectively. This includes learning and detailing all the information and skills and recalling them. Information decays and degrades over the period of time and needs to be replenished often.

At times one information supercedes another information and is well retained than the first one. At times it is observed that people tend to forget information due to stress or pressure for e.g. during exams howsoever well read the student is but gets nervous and forgets the answer. These are short-term memory loss as in most cases the memory springs back rather than being lost forever.

In women pregnancy also affects their memory due to the hormonal changes that occur in their body. Due to biological changes in their body women suffer from stress and tension and this leads to the neuron settings in their brain being disturbed. But they usually overcome that thru the supplements or post pregnancy.

The Memory of the Mind

Have you ever heard someone say an elephant never forgets? Maybe someone you know was compared to an elephant in a similar way, as in having the memory of an elephant. The mind of an animal can be substantially large in its learning capacity, using memory to perform amazingly in many ways.

The mind can shut down memory, temporarily or permanently, depending on whether or not what it endured was a traumatic event that the mind just refuses to access or a scant bump to the head. People have protected themselves subconsciously by disengaging the memory. The mind sometimes seems to play tricks on us by confusing one memory with another. Sometimes this causes the person to be unable to function in society. What seems to be a problem with memory can actually be a problem with the processing of information going into the mind.

Prescription medicines can sometimes affect the memory, especially if you choose to combine a dangerous mixture. Even over-the-counter medications have to be closely monitored in their ability to work well with each other or with certain prescription medications. Prescription medications can also improve your ability to use your memory, clearing up other health problems that might interfere with your mind's performance.

The mind is complex in its capabilities, but without memory it cannot perform even the simplest of tasks. The body depends on memory to function. How would we brush our teeth if we couldn't remember the process of adding the toothpaste, wetting the toothbrush, putting it in our mouths, scrubbing the teeth, and the rinsing? Such daily tasks are overlooked in importance because they become mundane repetitions in our memory. A person who is preoccupied may not even recall the task of brushing the teeth.

Animals have a sense that allows them to remember whether or not a person has been cruel to them. They may store the information in their memory and act upon it at a later time, sometimes unsuspectingly getting their revenge. A dog being trained for police work has to remember which person in uniform is its master. It has to retain enough information to perform acceptably in each working, many times dangerous, situation. The dog has to remember many types of scents and commands.

Miniature horses have been trained to lead the blind around noisy, busy environments. The horse must have adequate memory to pass the necessary requirements to be a guide animal. The blind person's life depends upon the memory of the miniature horse every day and night for as long as they are together.

A blind person must have the ability to use other senses besides their eyes. Their memories have to be capable of helping them function in their own homes. If something is out of place, their routines will suffer, and possibly an injury will occur.

The memory is the storage capacity of the mind. Often neglected, often unappreciated until something occurs to help us take notice of just how important it is to our well-being.

The Study of Memory Improvement

There has been more than one study on how to improve memory and reasons for memory loss. Let's review some causes for impaired memory.

Suppose you decide you need help enduring a nerve-racking airplane ride, so you swallow one of the calming, hypnotic prescription drugs designed for insomniacs and sufferers of panic attacks or anxiety. These are drugs like alprazolam, triazolam, or zolpidem. (One well-known drug that has become more popular just in the past few years is Ambien.) Unfortunately, a side effect of such a drug is a condition also known as 'traveler amnesia'.

Normally, once a person stops the use of the prescription drug that caused the amnesia, memory begins to improve. Even though you should always be aware of the side effects of any drug, it is possible that something new will develop that wasn't discovered in the study of the drug. Also, because each person is unique, a drug may cause a reaction only one person may experience.

Another study done on memory loss involves head trauma. This can lead to transient post concussive syndrome. Symptoms are mental dullness, poor memory, depressed mood, and headaches. These symptoms can last a few days or a few weeks. Often after a tragedy such as a vehicle accident that causes extensive head injury, the resulting concussion brings immediate mental confusion.

Other ways to obtain head trauma include hitting a head during a hard fall, something heavy falling on the head, or someone hitting your head with a hard object (accidentally, or during a fight).

There have been a large number of studies done regarding memory impairment caused by diseases or psychological problems. With a disease there is hope of improvement, depending on how far the disease has progressed before proper help was obtained. Also, science and technology constantly allow more information to be discovered. As for psychological problems, there is treatment for the underlying problems through psychiatric care, counseling, and medication. Often the memory can be used as a healing tool against itself, such as through reliving an event to better understand why memories were blocked.

An important thing to understand in many cases of memory impairment is that repetition may be crucial to positive progress. We must teach ourselves to do something over and over until we can unconsciously remember because of habit. Some people are creatures of habit and can only get through their days with the most success if they stick to their routines. Anything that deviates from their routine can cause anxiety and throw their mental balance off course significantly. Their routine becomes their mental and emotional security blanket.

Several types of animals have been used in laboratories as a basis to study memory improvement. Hence the old mouse in a maze routine! Dogs can be taught to win contests by their abilities to remember and follow set courses with obstacles. Orangutans have been taught to learn sign language because of their ability to grasp and remember. Lost cats have found their way home after extensive travel. So, the study of memory continues to amaze and confound science and the medical world!

What Can I Do for Memory Improvement?

There are several outside forces that can affect one's memory. As has been found in many other areas, diet is one link to impairing memory. Another well-known affecter of our memory is lack of physical exercise. Of course, there are foreign substances we put into our unsuspecting bodies, such as drugs or alcohol, even prescription drugs can have a negative effect. Injuries or traumatic events can affect memories, as can diseases. Inadequate mental and indeed even spiritual stimulation has long been known to damage our minds, bodies and emotions.

Let's explore the life stressors in connection with memory impairment. If you have a life that is in turmoil on a daily basis, unorganized and over packed with activities, never allowing yourself adequate care, your memory is certain to develop some degree of suffering. It is surely something that will require some thought and time to repair. You must first take stock of your priorities. How well do you care for your mind and body? Maybe you think a quick rush to the gym will do the trick. The key here is 'rush'.

Rushing around is one area where we cause our mental health to suffer. Long-term turmoil is not our friend, and rushing is something that can become an unwelcome habit. Some people who crave a smoother, more relaxing routine have to actually be taught how to achieve it because they have become so accustomed to rushing through their day.

There may be more than one area you'll have to change in your life to obtain memory improvement. One important step to healthy memory function is to get more oxygen to your brain. Proper blood flow and plenty of oxygen are two factors that must not be overlooked. You can achieve these by learning breathing exercises. This can help clear your mind, give it a boost, and relieve stress. Even if it is only temporary, it is still an important step in beginning your journey to memory improvement.

Another important step to improvement is eating properly. A well-rounded diet can benefit in many ways, and often the benefits to memory function are overlooked. The diet can affect the physical health, obviously. But if you aren't in good physical health, how can you also be in the best health mentally? The mind depends on the body to work at its best for the mind to work well.

What about the living environment? Can a dirty home affect your memory? Maybe it sounds absurd, but yes, it can. If your senses are constantly subjected to anything negative, it will begin to affect your brain health. A clean home doesn't just look better, it can increase your happiness and sense of peace, which will in turn calm you and allow your mind and memory to focus on more productive thoughts.

Not only does the sight of your clean home allow improvement in your life, the smell of a clean home can be uplifting as well. So, bring out those candles or potpourri, room sprays, and cleaning supplies!

What Goes In Must Find A Way Out

There has been a story written about a lady who suffered a traumatic experience. She went into a coma, never expected to return to reality as we know it. Her reality became a recollection of stories written by a well-known author of many years past. Her mind lived in the stories she had read. This was discovered because she did occasionally speak, but not in conversation or in response. She spoke sentences from the stories, never more, never less.

The memory is complex, often misunderstood and underrated. People who suffer from coma, psychological complexities, children with learning disabilities, and people who get amnesia are often a mental mystery. Amnesia confounds those who watch a friend or loved one who suffers from it.

No one can ever really know how much someone in a coma can hear, understand, and remember. Children are often misunderstood before being diagnosed with a particular learning disability. Someone with a brain tumor may have plenty of information stored in their memories that eventually becomes too muddled to process. They lose their ability to make sense of the memories they contain.

Social phobia is another crippler of memory. When put in the spotlight, a person can become physically distressed, sometimes severely suffering by having anxiety or panic attacks. It is embarrassing to say the least. The confidence level drops dramatically, making it extremely hard to overcome this fear. But it is an irrational fear, and there is hope. A determined person can be taught to overcome a phobia such as this by putting themselves in situations that allow for gradual building of confidence. Each small step towards recovery is a step towards a stronger self-esteem and opens the door to endless opportunities. Thus, the memory loss connected to such can eventually become something the person is able to joke about. This, in turn, can put others at ease, who have suffered the same set-backs, and give them hope and courage to laugh at their fear.

Anytime a person is put on the spot, it can cause temporary memory loss. Singing in front of a church congregation, however small, can make a person feel as though the whole world is watching and waiting for them to make a mistake. Giving an oral book report in class can terrify young children. Stage fright can cripple a potential acting career. It is possible that a person can overcome such paranoia with coaching and the willpower to succeed.

If you are faced with making an impression in a work environment, the embarrassment of forgetting a name could become the basis for teasing at your expense. Try some helpful word association. Learn to choose words that describe new people you meet to help you recall their names. An example would be "Silly Sally" or "Hyper Henry". All it takes is some effort and tricks to strengthen your ability to remember. Practice and dedication are the keys. Eventually, what goes in will find it much easier to make its way back out!

Why Would You 'Memorize'?

The English language is a complex language in the way that it makes words sound different from the way they are spelled. The meanings can vary greatly as well, but the spelling can be a bigger challenge.

The word memory has several different words associated with it, such as memories, memorization, memorize, memo, memorandum, memorized, memorizing. Then you have words like mnemonic, which is of or helping the memory. The word remember, means recall, which is to bring back to the memory. Recollect means remember.

But the spelling itself may confuse someone. Some people mistakenly spell the word memorize with an s, as in 'memorize'. They both sound similar. After all, the word sunrise is spelled with an s. Then you have the saying, 'rise and shine'. The word horizon is spelled with a z. Confused yet? It's completely understandable! There's the word arouse, spelled with an s. Mesozoic is spelled with both the s and the z, as is mesmerize. Magazine uses the z. So, if you misspell the word and use 'memorize' instead, don't worry. Many people confuse the spelling.

No wonder it is hard for some children (and adults who speak another language) to memorize spelling! It is a wonder a search engine can find the words you want in the correct spelling. But the wonderful thing about search engines is, even if you spell the word memorize instead of the correct way, the wonderfully knowledgeable computer can work its magic and send you in the right direction!

The brain has to process a ton of information just in the early phases of learning. To exercise and improve the memory is one of the most beneficial processes of getting to the next phases of life, education, and business (later on, of course). Some say that a babe in the womb can exercise its memory by the mother's use of classical music during its development. It stimulates the mind, which stimulates the learning process, and memory is the key to the learning process. Some mothers-to-be will play educational tapes or cds to their unborn children.

Some people encourage the memory process by listening to recordings while they sleep. There have been students who listen to their studies while they sleep. Some attempt to learn another language this way.

Hypnosis can help in this way as well, to those who are susceptible to such. There are programs that use hypnosis to help people stop smoking and lose weight, and gain self-confidence. It embeds the information in the self-conscious, so the mind will remember and use it when necessary.

Beepers are invented to help find lost keys, tape recorders are used in class to help recall important information for passing tests, memo pads sell every day in office supply stores. So, don't despair if you have a little trouble remembering how to spell.

Try using a recording while you sleep to get your memory in top shape and enhance your spelling abilities. Try taking a seminar on memory, reading books on the subject, watching videos, or grab a friend and take a class together. The memory is the key to success.

Download 100+ Books
Completely Free!
No Hassles...
No Charges...
Just Click And Download
100% Free!
CLICK HERE

Learn The Art Of Leaving
Your Physical Body!

Download Today!

ASTRAL PROJECTION

ASTRAL PROJECTION
Amazing Journeys
Outside Your Body
Abhishek Agarwal

"Learn The Closely Guarded Secrets Of Safely
Leaving Your Physical Body And Traveling Anywhere
You Want To! Learn How To Get Free From Your
Physical Body Limitations... Within 30-60 Days!"

DOWNLOAD NOW

This Product Is Brought To You By